WHO AM I?

Who am I?

I am graceful and galloping, strong and swift.
I live in a stable.

WHO AM I?

By Moira Butterfield
Illustrated by Wayne Ford

Belitha Press

First published in the UK in 2000 by

Belitha Press Limited, London House,
Great Eastern Wharf, Parkgate Road,
London SW11 4NQ

ISBN 1 84138 105 5

British Library Cataloguing in Publication Data for this book
is available from the British Library.

Printed in Hong Kong

Editor: Stephanie Bellwood
Designer: Helen James
Illustrator: Wayne Ford / Wildlife Art Agency
Consultant: Jock Boyd

My hoofs are hard.
My legs are long.
I'm fast and friendly, big and strong.
I gobble apples,
grass and hay.
Then I lift my head and neigh.

Who am I?

Here is my eye.

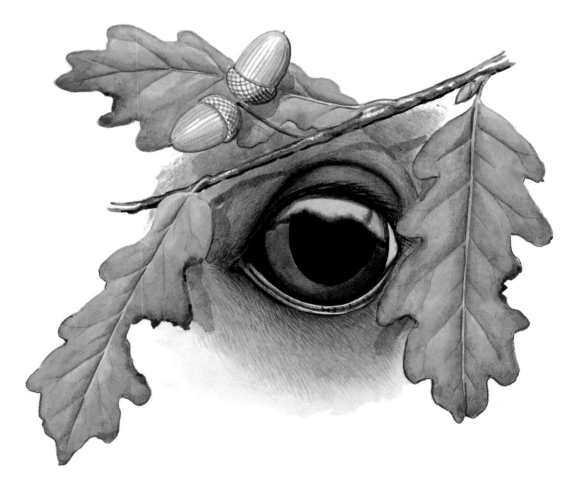

I stand in my field
and look at the
animals nearby.
How many sheep
can you see?

If I see something
that makes me feel
scared or angry,
I roll my eyes and
make my ears lie flat.

Here are my teeth.

I use them to nibble plants. I like to eat the grass in my field. Sometimes my owner gives me hay to eat.

I love to munch sweet foods. I gobble up apples and grind them with my teeth.

Here are my legs.

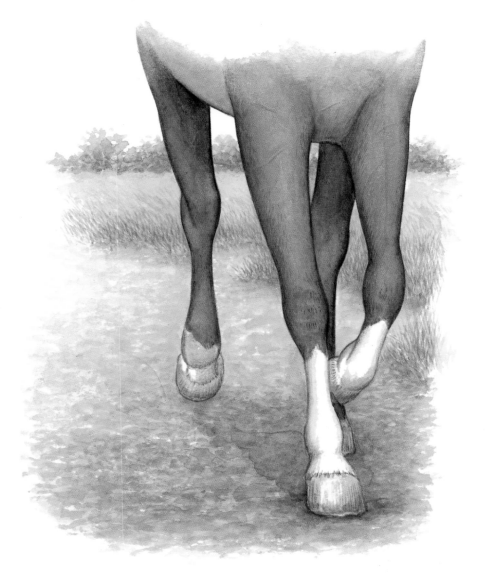

I can walk, trot
or gallop along.
If I am angry, watch
out! I kick hard
with my back legs.

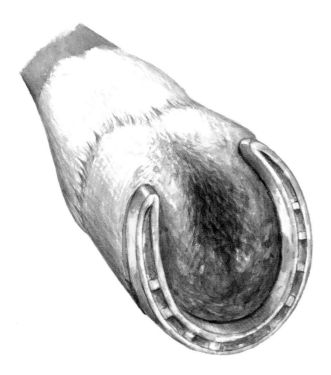

I have four hard
hoofs. Each hoof
has a metal shoe
fitted underneath
to protect it.

Here is my mane.

It helps to keep
me warm in winter.
If the weather is
bad I stay indoors
in my cosy stable.

In summer I stand
outside in the sun.
I shake my mane
and flick my tail
to get rid of flies.

Here is my skin.

I am covered in soft, smooth hair. My owner cleans and brushes me. This is called grooming.

I am a red colour called chestnut. Not all animals like me are red. What colours can you see?

Here is my nose.

When I have been galloping I breathe hard through my nostrils. It looks as if steam is coming out of them.

I am good at smelling things. I like to sniff other animals. If you came near I would smell you, too.

Here is my head.

I have a special way of saying hello.
I stretch out my neck,

open my mouth and...
neigh!

Have you guessed who I am?

I am a horse.

Point to my...

long mane

strong legs

large nostrils

pointed ears

swishing tail

hard hoofs

I am a female horse.
I am called a mare.

Here is my baby.

He is called a foal.
His thin legs are
wobbly at first,
but he soon
learns to stand.

My foal loves to
play in the field.
He rolls, kicks and
runs. I stay close
to him all the time.

Here is my home.

I live on a farm where there
are stables and grassy fields.

Can you see me in the picture?
Look for two foals and three sheep.

Here are some other kinds of horses.

◄ This is a Shetland Pony. It is very small with a shaggy mane.

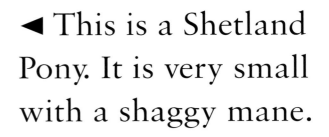

► Pinto horses have large markings on their coat, mane and tail.

Some horses are working animals.
Big, strong horses can pull
carts and carry heavy loads.

Can you answer these questions about me?

What do I like to eat?

How does my owner protect my hoofs?

Where do I live?

What is my baby called?

What happens when I am angry or scared?

What noise do I make?

Can you name some kinds of horses?

How do I get rid of flies in summer?

What do I do when I meet another animal?

Here are some words to learn about me.

chestnut A reddish-brown colour.

gallop To run fast.

grooming Brushing and cleaning a horse to keep it looking neat.

hay Dried grass. I like to eat hay because it tastes sweet.

hoof My hard foot.

mane The long, shaggy hair that grows along the top of my neck.

mare A female horse over the age of four. A younger female horse is called a filly. Male horses over the age of four are called stallions, and young male horses are colts.

neigh The long, loud noise that I make. Can you neigh like me?

stable My cosy, warm, indoor home.

trot To walk quickly.